AMUSEMENT PARKS

Jim Hillman

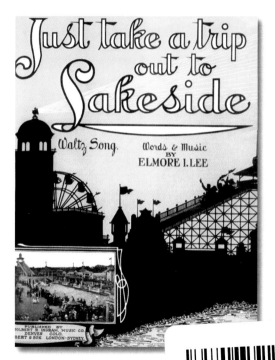

SHIRE PUBLICATIONS

Published in Great Britain in 2013 by Shire Publications Ltd, Midland House, West Way, Botley, Oxford OX2 0PH, United Kingdom.

43-01 21st Street, Suite 220B, Long Island City, NY 11101, USA.

E-mail: shire@shirebooks.co.uk   www.shirebooks.co.uk

A CIP catalogue record for this book is available from the British Library.

Shire Library no. 715.   ISBN-13: 978 0 74781 209 8

Jim Hillman has asserted his right under the Copyright, Designs and Patents Act, 1988, to be identified as the author of this book.

Designed by Tony Truscott Designs, Sussex, UK and typeset in Perpetua and Gill Sans.

Printed in China through Worldprint Ltd.

13 14 15 16 17   10 9 8 7 6 5 4 3 2 1

COVER IMAGE
Well-dressed patrons of New York's Coney Island anticipate the next of a steady flow of slide adventurers; people-watching was a popular diversion on America's early midways.

TITLE PAGE IMAGE
Lakeside Amusement Park in Denver, Colorado, is celebrated in this cover panel to Elmore Lee's "Just Take a Trip out to Lakeside" waltz sheet music.

CONTENTS PAGE IMAGE
A coaster train travels the lift hill of a traditional wooden roller coaster. The anticipation of cresting the hill is almost as exciting as the actual ride.

ACKNOWLEDGEMENTS
I want to thank John Murphy for his friendship, support with technology, and encouraging words. I also want to express appreciation to all my friends within the amusement park and enthusiast communities, especially Jim Abbate, Craig Burda, Rick Davis, and Jim Futrell. Don Helbig (Kings Island), Ralph Lopez (National Amusement Park Historical Association), Pete Owens (Dollywood), Tom Spackman and Sherry Vogel (Indiana Beach), Pat Koch and Paula Werne (Holiday World), and the staff at Cincinnati's Coney Island, all made significant contributions, along with others too numerous to mention; a debt is owed to the caretakers of America's amusement parks, as well as to the work of other researchers and who have come before me. Most importantly, I want to acknowledge the love and support of my family, especially my wife Kathy. Finally, I am thankful for the continuing support of the University of Phoenix, where I serve as an adjunct faculty member.

PHOTO CREDITS
I would also like to thank those organizations which have allowed me to use the following illustrations: National Amusement Park Historical Association, page 12 (right) and page 19; and MPL Music Publishing (top). All other photographic reproductions and park items come from the author's personal collection.

CONTENTS

GENESIS

MAYBE THE AROMAS are what first grab your attention: an odd combination of fried foods, fresh flowers, whipped cotton candy, the heat rising from the asphalt walkways, the coaster grease, and an unidentified smell or two. It could be the sounds that get you. You hear the band organ music of the carousel, the giggles and screams of excited children, the hawkers working the games of chance, and the clicking and clanking of the roller coaster trains on the way to the crest of the lift hill. There are lights everywhere, some flashing, some changing colors. There are unique buildings with numerous signs, and strange moving machines going in multiple directions, seemingly at once. You feel excited yet apprehensive as you enter the gates of the amusement park.

Those very sensations have been experienced by those of us fortunate enough to have visited America's amusement parks. The origination of the amusement industry in the United States was not an organized progression. Evolving from humble picnic grounds and gathering spots, recreational opportunities grew and mirrored counterparts on other continents.

The sixteenth and seventeenth centuries saw rapid growth of European towns and the corresponding crowdedness of communal living, punctuated by dismal, smoky industry, unsavory sanitary conditions, and general bleakness. Newly emerging pleasure gardens offered an oasis to those city dwellers desiring a simple, convenient escape from urban life. As immediate predecessors to the traditional American amusement park, the pleasure gardens of Europe grew to include simple diversions such as open areas for community socializing, developed swimming areas, dancing halls, games of chance, exhibitionist entertainment, and primitive, often animal-powered rides.

The masses flocked to the gardens to escape the pressures of urban life. But the very cities that nurtured the desire for escape eventually accelerated the decline and near disappearance of these European play lands. By the close of the politically unstable eighteenth century, few of the gardens survived. Dyrehavsbakken in Copenhagen, Denmark, and Prater in Vienna, Austria, are the two remaining examples of those wonderful gardens.

Opposite:
This collage shows ride tickets and trinkets from a variety of operating and defunct parks. Early European parks, as well as the well-known Coney Island in Brooklyn, New York, have greatly influenced the modern American amusement park industry.

Artistic sideshow banners have become a familiar sight on Coney Island midways, harkening back to the days when exhibitionist displays were common entertainment at European pleasure gardens.

A Coney Island midway hawker, as seen in the late 1990s, attracts a customer for Reynolds' Believe It You're Nuts Hysterical Museum. Bobby Reynolds remains the last of the great sideshow showmen on the sawdust trail.

Similar to the gardens across the pond, but well before the advent of multimillion-dollar, corporate-owned, and profit-focused theme parks, simple pleasure gardens dotted the American landscape. Jones Woods, located in New York along the East River near Manhattan, is documented as America's first major amusement area. From the early 1800s, the Woods expanded from a simple gathering spot to include then-novel amenities such as a designated picnic area, donkey rides, and even a bustling beer hall.

Across America, but mostly concentrated along the east coast, small and primitive resorts began to appear in fields and tree groves in or around developing cities, usually near bodies of water or areas known for their natural beauty. Of upmost significance, the grand entrepreneurial experiment known as Coney Island took shape on a small sliver of land-hugging Brooklyn, New York. Located adjacent to the largest concentration of people in America, this seaside peninsula was ripe for development. The first hotel was built and accepted visitors in 1829, capitalizing on the soothing ocean waves and smooth sands of the nearby beach. By the mid-1800s, bathing, dining, dancing, and other recreational facilities were actively in use, and rail service was supplied to the blooming resort area. Before long, the working man's paradise was brimming with more sophisticated entertainment offerings and often questionable diversions.

The ocean breeze blew forth vaudeville and cabaret theaters alongside the crystal balls of fortunetellers, street sideshow hawkers, pickpockets, and medicine men touting their tonics. The 300-foot Iron Tower, relocated from the 1876 Philadelphia Centennial Exposition, was erected on the peninsula in 1877, and in 1884, the world's first traditional wooden roller coaster, invented by LaMarcus Thompson, was constructed. Known as the Switchback Railway, this new attraction encouraged numerous businessmen to invest in the Brooklyn area known as Coney Island; the peninsula was becoming a local retreat and regional vacation destination. It is not an exaggeration to state that most people had heard talk of Coney Island.

Sea Lion Park, which later evolved into Luna Park, was the first true, gated amusement park in Coney Island. Beginning an unrivaled Coney tradition in 1895, Sea Lion Park was a showplace of both tried and tested ideas, including a water chute ride centerpiece, and of the new and exciting, such as the Flip Flap, one of the first looping American coasters. Augmenting the rides, a renowned sea lion show gave credence to the park's name and foreshadowed the addition of themed shows to the park's entertainment offerings.

This postcard from 1906 shows several classic images, including scenes of all three major Coney Island parks: Luna, Dreamland, and Steeplechase. Among the depictions are shots of the Iron Pier, the Johnstown Flood attraction, and famous Surf Avenue.

COPYRIGHT 1906 ILLU'S POST CARD & NOV CO. N.Y.

7

The popularity of Coney Island, especially the beach, is accurately depicted here. The famous Steeplechase Parachute Tower and funhouse are shown in the background.

Luna Park in Coney Island was known for exciting diversions. One of the most popular attractions was the Helter Skelter slide. Note that the clientele is dressed well for a day at the park.

With the success of Sea Lion Park, Coney Island restaurant operator George Tilyou opened a competing venue, Steeplechase Park. This new park featured the signature Steeplechase ride, a simulated horse race along a line-up of eight parallel tracks with wooden horses that resembled carousel horses. In 1904, Dreamland Park opened across the street from Luna Park, complete with elaborate fountains and floral arrangements, fascinating electric lights, and unique attractions. The Coney Island triad of parks—Luna, Steeplechase, and Dreamland—was complete.

Complementing and expanding upon the successful amusement parks within the district, a few state-of-the-industry attractions constructed during this heyday time still remain, including the Wonder Wheel (1920), Cyclone (1927), and the Steeplechase Park Parachute Jump tower, which was constructed in 1939 for the New York World's Fair and later moved to Coney Island in 1941. While the Parachute Drop is nonoperational, the 262-foot structure remains as an iconic landmark. The Cyclone wooden coaster is now part of Luna Park, a revitalization endeavor that pays homage in moniker to the original park, while the Wonder Wheel still twirls riders, along with an assortment of carnival-style rides, at Deno's Wonder Wheel Amusement Park.

Behind this modest, locked gate stands one of the most iconic symbols of Coney Island: the Wonder Wheel.

The Wonder Wheel is more than just an amusing Coney Island icon. The 400,000-pound steel Wonder Wheel of the Eccentric Ferris Wheel Company became an official New York City landmark in 1989. Sixteen enclosed units slide on roller coaster-like rails between the central wheel hub and the rims; six stationary cars are affixed to the rim. Full-size replicas of the wheel can be found at Disney's California Adventure Park, as well as at a facility

The Wonder Wheel, named an official New York City landmark in 1989, towers 150 feet over Coney Island. The massive wheel, containing 100 percent Bethlehem steel, weighs 400,000 pounds. Built in 1920, the ride can accommodate 144 passengers at a time.

German immigrant Charles Feltman is credited with bringing the hotdog to America, selling his novelty food on the streets of Coney Island. The legacy of Coney Island hotdogs is still proudly served at Nathan's Famous, founded by Nathan Handwerker in 1916.

in Yokohama, Japan. The Wonder Wheel has maintained an excellent safety record. It has been continuously operated every scheduled day without fail except during the Great New York City Blackout on July 13, 1977. When the power failed, the great wheel was hand-cranked until all passengers were safely on the ground.

Countless people of all ages have ridden the Wonder Wheel as well as the numerous other rides on Coney Island. But Coney Island is technically neither a pleasure garden nor an amusement park. Rather, it is an amusement area within Brooklyn. The Coney Island neighborhood consisted of numerous independently owned and operated attractions, and even entire amusement parks were built within the area. As amusement parks were developed in other parts of the country, park owners would often emulate the Coney Island model of development, relying upon independent concessionaires to bring their amusements into the park. Park owners would charge the concessionaires for space in their parks and possibly a percentage of attraction revenue. Amusement park owners were then able to constantly expand their facilities without much direct investment, while keeping properties fresh with the newest and most unique attractions. In this respect, Coney Island became the queen of all amusement parks. The newest and most unique amusements were introduced at Coney Island and, if successful, replicated elsewhere by an expanding cadre of concessionaires.

Coney Island continued to flourish as the nation grew, but popularity began to diminish after World War II. Blue-collar, working-class Brooklyn was dealing with the symptoms of urban blight, which filtered through its neighborhoods, including Coney Island, which began to suffer from years of falling revenues and deteriorating infrastructures. Vandalism, a string of devastating fires, ocean pollution, shifting American leisure preferences, competition, and many other factors led to its decline. Classy vaudeville and the newest mechanical lures gave way to whatever the independent concessionaires and park owners supplied, which often devolved into cheesy burlesque clubs, portable carnival rides, and flea market retail.

The closing of Steeplechase Park in 1964 all but sealed the fate of Coney Island. By the 1970s, the area was no longer a safe place to visit, especially after dark. Prostitutes, drug dealers, and gangs replaced the couples, families, and children who once strolled along the midways. There were no real plans for sustainability, let alone revitalization and growth, and efforts for continuity within this amusement community were mostly unenforceable. The scales of balance between amusement and tawdriness had been tipped.

While not much remains of the original Coney Island, intervening years have brought new life to the area. With government support, new investments, including a baseball stadium and new, high-tech coasters and rides, are gaining the continued attention of area residents and visitors alike. New tourism promotions and events, building upon the popularity of Coney Island's annual Mermaid Parade, are bringing families back to the boardwalk. Although the atmosphere has been updated and sanitized, and most early attractions are long since lost, the spirit of the once great resort can again be heard in the excited screams of a new generation.

This picture postcard montage shows several Coney Island scenes. In the years to follow, Coney Island would struggle through years of urban decay, including the destruction and abandonment of several popular attractions.

BEYOND CONEY ISLAND

AROUND THE SAME TIME Coney Island was developing, an amusement park was taking root in Bristol, Connecticut, on Gad Norton's farm. Because large crowds had gathered at the farm on numerous occasions, including a well-publicized and attended explosives demonstration, Norton determined that a need existed for a community gathering place. Dubbed "Lake Compounce" by Norton, the farm became grounds for community events, picnics, and water activities. The tradition continues today as Lake Compounce is America's oldest continuously operating amusement park.

Not that reaching that status has been easy: Lake Compounce has had to battle challenging economic climates and ownership changes. But even during the early 1990s when the park was unable to open for a whole season, the grounds would open for at least a few days to secure the longevity claim. While most of the park rides were not operational during this time period, entertainment was booked to get patrons to the park. Even with numerous hardships, Lake Compounce has survived and continues to add new attractions, targeting families and preserving an important part of American amusement park history.

But for every success, there are losses. In nearby Warwick, Rhode Island, Rocky Point Park, established in 1847, was not as fortunate and closed in 1995. This perennial favorite continues to be missed—much like the hundreds of similar parks that emerged following the Civil War.

In the years following the War Between the States, cities grew and a need for cost-effective mass transit emerged. The solution was electric-powered trolleys, with lines running from the central city areas to population outskirts. The trolley lines proved popular, serving the transportation needs of the working class. People heavily utilized the trolleys during workweek days, but evening and weekend ridership was virtually nonexistent. Given that electricity was new and expensive and prices fluctuated without governmental regulation, the electric railway companies began establishing amusement areas at the end of the trolley lines to encourage evening and weekend ridership.

Opposite: Depiction of the Flying Turns on the cover of a National Amusement Park Historical Association special publication honoring the classic ride.

These amusement park areas were essentially trolley parks, existing solely to encourage ridership. Some of these trolley parks were simply picnic parks, but others began to add amenities like restaurants, dance halls, penny arcades, and performance areas, while others added a few mechanical rides. No matter what the trolley companies built, the overall business practice was successful, and numerous small play lands were built around America.

In addition to the trolley companies, food and beverage distributors, breweries, and prospecting entrepreneurs that demonstrated interest in America's appetite for leisure, the municipality of Westchester County, New York, carefully planned a well-designed urban park bordering Long Island Sound's shoreline. In 1928, this area, on the outskirts of Rye, New York, became Playland, developed from acquired, dated amusements located along the strip. A swimming beach, bathing house, picturesque boardwalk, and ice rink soon complemented the park. Art deco architecture, electric lights, and neon displays accentuated the Aeroplane coaster and milder Dragon coaster, which anchored the park.

While trolley parks were primarily simple and small, exposition parks were developed on a much grander scale and modeled after world's fairs. Coney's Luna Park is often referred to as the first of the permanent exposition or electric parks, while the Island's Dreamland was perhaps the most detailed and grand. Because electric lighting was not yet commonplace, the general public found the elaborate buildings outlined in electric lights fascinating. As the forerunner to today's modern theme parks, exhibition parks promoted intricate exhibits that were their cornerstones, attractions

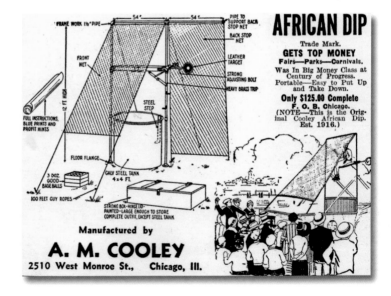

In the early 1900s, many amusement parks were referred to as white cities, aptly named given the majority of these parks catered only to a white clientele. The African Dip was a midway game demonstrating discriminatory practices.

This opening panel to the official visitor's guide to Denver, Colorado's Lakeside Park shows the grand electric tower. Lakeside Park was also known as the White City as displayed within the logo; minorities were not allowed in the park during the early years of operation.

that transported the public from mundane urban life to exciting exotic locales. Famous exhibition parks included Boston's Wonderland, Cleveland's Luna Park, and Indianapolis's Wonderland.

White City, an exhibition park in Chicago, opened in 1905. The name referred not only to the park itself, but also to the desired clientele. Independent white cities soon opened around the country and solicited only white patronage. For the most part, early American amusement parks did not allow people of color admittance; the amusement park industry in America was highly segregated. Denver's Lakeside Park, still illuminated by a traditional lighted tower, opened in 1908 as White City, and remains as the only true exposition park left standing in America.

The Shooting Gallery, Fun House, and Rocket Ships ride as seen in this postcard of Lakeside Park's Fun Lane. This popular Denver, Colorado, park competed directly with nearby Elitch Gardens. While Elitch Gardens catered to the more affluent patron, Lakeside Park was seen more as a working man's playland.

Some amusement historians estimate that as many as 1,500 parks were operating in America by the mid-1900s. This was truly the golden age of the American amusement park. While there were plenty of exposition and trolley parks, most parks were smaller and offered a shaded picnic grove and

Lakeside Park's Rocket Ship ride and Photomation booth are long gone. Attractions similar to the Rocket Ship ride could be found at many American amusement parks, but none remain in operation.

occasional entertainment, often resembling municipal parks, with rides added as an afterthought. Americans would go to the parks, often in fancy dress, to socialize and relax, to enjoy the gardens, to sip a cold drink, and to linger and people watch. The parks offered a respite from the growing infringements of city life.

As parks flourished and owners learned to cater to their clientele, increasing competition for leisure dollars and thrilling experiences created a cadre of ride designers and manufacturers. Rides were being mass-produced and distributed to various parks to meet the growing demand for new mechanical wonders.

Located in Coney Island, the William F. Mangels Company produced classic whip rides. Other ride manufacturers at the time included the Eli Bridge Company, which produced Ferris wheels, and the Philadelphia Toboggan Company, known for producing quality roller coasters and carousels. The Dayton Fun House Company, one of the largest mass producers of amusement rides, survived well into the 1980s as International Amusement Devices. The Dodgem Corporation brought bumper cars to America's midways in 1919, followed by the beloved Tumble Bugs (1925), and Tilt-a-Whirls (1926). In 1926, the Pretzel Amusement Company popularized dark rides, where electric ride vehicles would travel a single rail through a variety of interior, themed environments. Early dark rides were often referred to as ghost ships due to their supernatural themes. While only a handful of Bugs and Pretzels remain in traditional American parks, Tilt-a-Whirls

The Haunted House at Guntown Mountain was manufactured by Funni-Frite and may be the last operational Funni-Frite walkthrough in the United States. The Darkride and Funhouse Enthusiast membership consistently ranks this haunted attraction as one of America's most historic funhouse attractions.

An early postcard depicts a popular dark walkthrough attraction known as Noah's Ark. The funhouse-style attraction featured a large wooden ark rocking back and forth on a stone base. In America, only Kennywood Park in Pennsylvania still has an ark in operation.

are plentiful, well represented in permanent parks and traveling carnivals. Stationary, walkthrough funhouses, many having a Noah's Ark theme, were also common.

While not new to amusement parks, roller coasters were changing as well. During the early part of the 1900s, several novel coasters were constructed. Riverview Park in Chicago, for example, built the Potsdam Railway, which included cars suspended below the coaster tracks.

Many designers were working on looping contraptions and ways to make coasters faster and more thrilling. Originally known as scenic railways, coasters would provide a brakeman who rode the coaster train along with the ride's patrons. The brakeman controlled the speed of the train and monitored

Laffland at New York's Sylvan Beach is a dark ride manufactured by the Pretzel Company. The ride contains many original stunts in operational condition. This image shows National Amusement Park Historical Association members gathered just prior to awarding a plaque to the park.

A brightly colored tumble bug ride is seen at the defunct Whalom Park near Boston.

This cover of the National Amusement Park Historical Association's *NAPHA News* shows the first Virginia Reel at Massachusetts's Revere Beach in operation in 1910. The upper portion of the Pitt funhouse is visible in the background.

weather conditions, adjusting the brakes as needed, which greatly affected both the riding experience and general safety. With no wheels under the tracks and no track-braking mechanisms, nothing stopped the coaster trains from flying off the tracks except for the skills of the brakemen.

According to one coaster patent, "Each car will travel along the straight portions of the track and acquire a quick centrifugal motion in passing around the curves, turns or corners, the suddenness of which causes agitation or commotion of the occupants, and hence much merriment and amusement!" None of these coasters remain in the United States, although a handful exist abroad, including the scenic railway at Great Yarmouth Pleasure Beach, England, and the pleasure ride at Luna Park, Australia.

Along with the scenic railways, side friction coasters operated in several locations. There were still no wheels under the tracks; however, brakemen were not necessary. The coaster cars or trains breezed through troughs with bumper side plates keeping the cars on track. Side friction coasters are tame

NAPHA News
Volume 30 2008 Number 2

by modern standards, and the general design was not conducive to height or speed.

One of the greatest side friction coasters ever built in the United States was constructed in Anderson, Indiana, a dual-track monstrosity named Leap-the-Dips, which circled an Indian burial mound. The rurally located ride only ran for a few years, demolished due to lack of ridership and controversy surrounding the ride's location. Area residents not accustomed to state-of-the-industry rides in their backyards—much less one towering over burial grounds—were never quite sure what to make of the attraction.

The most celebrated side friction roller coaster is also the world's oldest operating wooden coaster. The generically named Leap-the-Dips, constructed in 1902 by the E. Joy Morris Company, is listed on the National Register of Historic Places and in 1996 gained status as a National Historic Landmark. The coaster can be found at Lakemont Park in Altoona, Pennsylvania. Today, the ride is operated by the nonprofit Leap-the-Dips Preservation Foundation.

Leap-the-Dips was constructed in 1902 by the E. Joy Morris Company. The coaster is seen in this early 1900s postcard.

Coasters have long held a special place in the hearts of park goers. John Miller is credited with revolutionizing the coaster construction industry. Miller designed a safety ratchet system that prevented coaster trains from rolling backward on the lift hill in case of chain breakage or power loss. He also patented a new way to hold coaster trains on the track by placing wheels both above and below the coaster track; the under wheels would effectively

keep the cars on the track. This under friction construction allowed for the transformation of coasters from mild scenic railways to white-knuckle speed machines with steep drops nearly to the ground, flat curves, and speeds previously unseen. Miller was prolific until his death in 1941. The largest collection of his coasters still in operation can be found at Kennywood Park in West Mifflin, Pennsylvania, near Pittsburgh. Kennywood is caretaker to Miller's Jack Rabbit (1921), Thunderbolt (1924, since modified), and Racer (1927).

At the close of the 1920s, another coaster innovation appeared on the midways in the guise of the Flying Turns. Norman Bartlett, inspired by Olympic bobsledding, created troughs through which wheeled vehicles traveled freestyle. With no established tracking, the bobsled-style cars would offer riders a slightly different ride each time. While the first installation was at the defunct Lakeside Park in Dayton, Ohio, no original Flying Turns rides have survived in the United States; there are a few metal models on park midways, but the unique ride offered by wooden troughs has disappeared. Knoebels Amusement Resort in Elysburg, Pennsylvania, has spent millions of dollars and years trying to reconstruct a wooden-trough Flying Turns true to the original ride experience; the park promises that the Flying Turns will return to at least one American midway.

Pennsylvania's Lakemont is home to Leap-the-Dips, the oldest standing wooden roller coaster in America. This picture shows the historic coaster prior to restoration, which eventually reopened in 1999. Leap-the-Dips is the only operational side friction roller coaster in the United States.

HARD TIMES AND
OPPORTUNITIES

WHILE AMUSEMENTS PARKS were flourishing through the 1920s in the United States, great political and economic changes were on the horizon. America's Great Depression and the stock market crash of 1929 resulted in persistent unemployment. Many parks closed because the majority of Americans did not have money to spend on leisure. Park owners were likewise cash-strapped with little means to obtain capital for park stability, let alone growth. To get patrons to the parks, food giveaways were common, as were entertainment offerings, and free ride tickets were liberally distributed. Trolley parks allowed free transport to the parks. A decade would pass before America's amusement industry would regain solid footing, only to face the implications of World War II.

During these dark times, maintenance needs were not adequately addressed, and parks began to look shoddy. Burlesque entertainment offerings, sideshows, and other low-brow entertainment were booked to draw crowds, but their presence on the midways did little to attract the more affluent customers to the parks. Some parks began booking Big Band artists like Glen Miller and the Dorsey Brothers Orchestra, acts which drew in a more desirable clientele.

World War II presented additional obstacles, including gas rationing. Gas-powered rides were forced to sit idle. Potential patrons were unable to travel to the parks in private vehicles. To get people through the gates, many parks operated buses from urban centers and train stations to the parks. Trolley parks offered free trolley rides. Manufacturing resources also were trumped by military needs, so materials for new rides and parts to keep existing rides spinning and rolling were simply not available.

The upside of World War II was that people had spending money thanks in large part to war-industry jobs. Parks in urban areas with public transportation, parks located near industrial centers, and facilities near military bases prospered.

In relation to patrons from the military, many parks began catering to a new clientele. Military men, usually traveling in small groups, typically were looking for a different brand of entertainment. These soldiers were often far away from home and looking for companionship. Midway areas began offering dime-a-dance attractions where servicemen could go into the park's ballroom, pick a young lady, and enjoy a dance or two. Professional escorts, even prostitutes, could be found on some midways, and beer halls and taverns became major amusement park attractions. While the soldiers were visiting amusement parks in droves, not many families, the traditional clientele attracted to the parks, were spending time or dollars in the parks.

When the troops returned home after the war, America experienced an unprecedented period of prosperity. Parks began the process of returning their facilities to meet the expectations of families. Flowers reappeared on the midways, and flesh shows were being replaced with family-friendly animal and magic shows. Maintenance needs were being addressed, and new attractions were being added. Because many amusement parks were unable to survive the Great Depression and the ramifications of World War II, far fewer competitors remained.

With this prosperity came shifting priorities, including escaping the inner cities and moving to the more relaxed suburbs. Because amusement parks were often located at the end of the disappearing trolley lines, they were essentially located in areas where people wanted to build their prefabricated suburban housing. Amusement parks were not typically desirable neighbors, and with rising property values, parks were being forced to close. Meanwhile, those parks that remained in America's inner cities faced the deterioration of adjacent neighborhoods. People who lived around the parks were no longer the more wealthy and affluent; that population had relocated to the suburbs.

Not all was bleak, however. As servicemen returned home, they bought new suburban homes and began planning for the future. A true baby boom was occurring, and perceptive entrepreneurs were formulating some

An Allan Herschell Kiddie coaster is seen thrilling the preschool crowd at the defunct Enchanted Forest Park in Chestertown, Indiana.

A compact layout of children's rides could once be found at Roger Williams Park in Providence, Rhode Island.

This promotional postcard shows an elevated shot of the defunct Sauzer's Amusement Park and Picnic Grove in Merrillville, Indiana. Many kiddielands added adult rides to increase appeal across demographics.

entertaining plans to cater to these young families. Kiddielands were blossoming in suburbs across the country. Kiddielands were small parks that catered exclusively to families with children under the age of ten. C. C. Macdonald opened the first kiddieland in San Antonio, Texas, in 1925. Prior to 1950, there were only a handful of kiddielands, but within a decade, there were more than 150 small kiddielands in America, most located near large cities. Many municipal parks, shopping centers, and even flea markets began offering small ride areas.

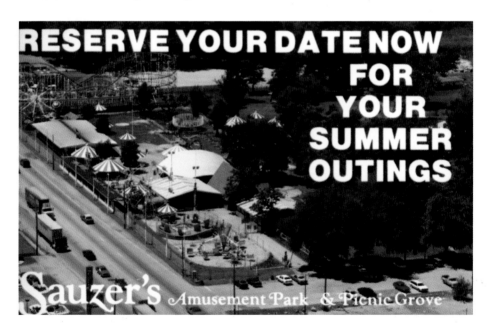

RESERVE YOUR DATE NOW FOR YOUR SUMMER OUTINGS

Sauzer's Amusement Park & Picnic Grove

To meet the demand for pint-sized attractions, Allan Herschell Company of North Tonawanda, New York, expanded from carousel manufacturing, prolifically producing 3,000 merry-go-rounds, to providing a variety of mass-manufactured children's rides. The Allan Herschell Company became known for packaging groups of children's rides together; these ride packages became known as kiddielands. The kiddieland market was popular and profitable; park owners and entrepreneurs enjoyed the convenience of purchasing these instant kiddielands.

The North Tonawanda manufacturing facility, while defunct, remains open as a museum that houses a collection of the company's smaller amusement rides. In later years, before merging with rival Chance Manufacturing in 1970, the Allan Herschell Company was noted for producing adult rides, including the popular Sky Wheel double Ferris wheel, Hurricane, and Twister, many of which are still in parks or on the traveling carnival circuit.

Most kiddielands were closed within a decade of opening. Along with the San Antonio Kiddie Park, though, a handful of kiddielands remain in operation. Memphis Kiddie Park caters to the birthday crowd on the outskirts of Cleveland, Ohio, while the Latham, New York, elementary

Kiddieland, the last traditional park in Chicago, closed in 2009. This park map from the last operating season shows how the park grew from a small children's park into a larger facility catering to families with both younger and older children.

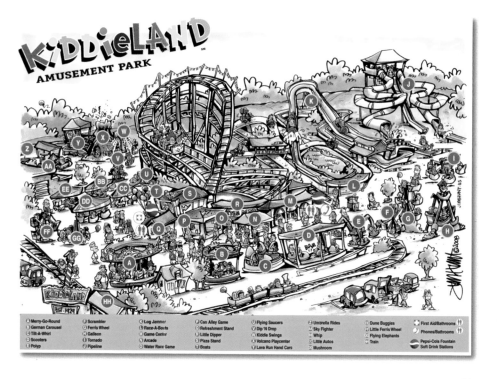

Merry-Go-Round	Scrambler	Log Jammer	Can Alley Game	Flying Saucers	Umbrella Rides	Dune Buggies	First Aid/Bathrooms
German Carousel	Ferris Wheel	Race-A-Bouts	Refreshment Stand	Dip 'N Drop	Sky Fighter	Little Ferris Wheel	Phones/Bathrooms
Tilt-A-Whirl	Galleon	Game Centr	Little Dipper	Kiddie Swings	Whip	Flying Elephants	
Scooters	Tornado	Arcade	Pizza Stand	Volcano Playcenter	Little Autos	Train	Pepsi-Cola Fountain
Polyp	Pipeline	Water Race Game	Boats	Lava Run Hand Cars	Mushroom		Soft Drink Stations

Uncle Donald and nephews tromp through the woods on their way to camp and fish at Disney's Animal Kingdom. Disney innovated the art of intricate themes within his parks.

The Monsanto Chemical Company exhibit was installed in Tomorrowland at California's Disneyland. Modern amusement park attractions are often sponsored by large companies.

school crowd can be found at Hoffman's Playland. Not quite a dozen of these historical parks are still in operation.

Concurrent with the rise and fall of kiddielands in America came the advent of the destination park, or theme parks. Walt Disney is given credit for popularizing the concept in America. Disney, however, did not develop the theme park concept. In fact, several parks embracing various themes were in operation prior to Disneyland's 1955 opening. Of the early theme parks, several remain in operation, including Knott's Berry Farm, formerly Ghost Town, in California (1940); Holiday World, formerly Santa Claus Land, in Indiana (1946); Santa's Workshop in New York (1949); Santa's Village in New Hampshire (1953); and Great Escape, formerly Storytown USA, also in New York (1954).

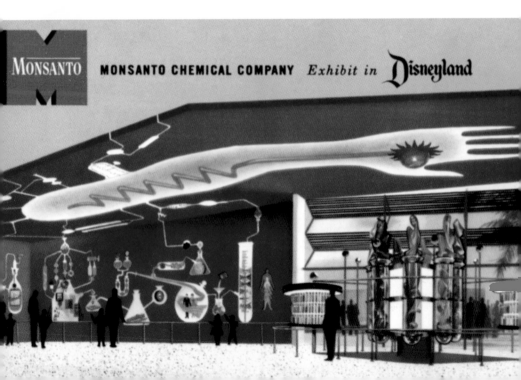

MONSANTO

MONSANTO CHEMICAL COMPANY *Exhibit in* Disneyland

THE THEME PARK CHALLENGE

THE MODERN THEME PARK raised the bar within the amusement industry with stress placed upon exquisitely manicured landscapes, exceptionally clean midways, and professional employees. Patricia Koch, director of values for Holiday World in Santa Claus, Indiana, said, "We run a family park. We listen and we care." It's a sentiment shared by many family parks.

In likewise fashion, the theme park industry was expected to focus on the guest experience, paying much credence to customer satisfaction. Because providing upscale amenities comes with a price, parks must rely on happy patrons and repeat patronage to fund the increased operational costs associated with themed experiences. Instead of marketing exclusively to local communities, theme parks saw their audience as regionally, or even nationally, based. Theme parks attempted to be true resorts worthy of America's vacation dollars.

Theme parks began evolving into gated attractions. While some continued to barter with ride tickets, most opted for the pay-one-price admission ticket. Paying one price at the gate was standardized by Pacific Ocean Park in California in the late 1950s, a failed themed endeavor partially funded by the CBS television network. By charging a gate admission, an amusement operator is better equipped to reduce

This early promotional brochure advertises Santa Claus Land in Santa Claus, Indiana. Santa Claus Land was one of the nation's first theme parks.

Official First Day Cover

Santa Claus Land

SANTA CLAUS IN
OCT
28
1983
47579

Seasons Greetings USA 20¢
FIRST DAY OF ISSUE

Santa Claus, Indiana 47579

Above: Santa Claus Land evolved into the Holiday World theme park. The Thanksgiving-themed area is seen with the Turkey Whirl scrambler entertaining visitors. The immense Voyage wooden coaster lift hill is seen in the background.

The Santa Claus, Indiana, post office sat on property adjacent to Santa Claus Land, now Holiday World; the post office, now relocated, still handles a large volume of seasonal letters to the jolly elf.

the number of unsavory characters who wander the midways without spending a dollar.

With Disneyland's success, solidified by opening-year attendance hitting the 4 million mark, several parks were immediately planned or rushed to open in the wake of Disney media hype. Most of these early attempts to ride the Disney wave were dismal failures. Magic Mountain (1958) near Denver began development, opened before completion, and closed abruptly in 1960, unfinished. Pleasure Island (1959) near Boston lasted a decade despite the fact that their signature animated, nonride attraction, Moby Dick, was always in a state of disrepair. Freedomland (1960) in the Bronx, New York, collapsed within four years of opening, having been poorly planned and shoddily constructed. Many smaller traditional parks began to give certain rides and attractions a theme, even giving whole areas of their parks a coherent identity,

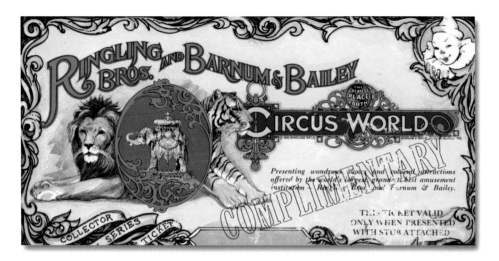

trying to pass themselves off as providing a theme park experience.

It was not until Six Flags over Texas (1961), located between Dallas and Fort Worth, that another large-scale theme park could truly be considered successful. Innovations led by the Six Flags brand include the introduction of the log flume ride and construction of the popular mine train-themed coasters. Sea World (1964), a novel aquatic life theme park in San Diego, was the next success story, followed by Walt Disney World (1971) in Florida, and country music park Opryland (1972), near Nashville. Six Flags also built new parks in the 1960s and '70s as the company attempted replication of Six Flags over Texas's success, bringing their brand of theme park entertainment to several other American markets.

Above: This ticket is from the defunct Circus World theme park in Florida. Later the park became Boardwalk and Baseball, another failed attempt to compete with the nearby Magic Kingdom.

Left: The Wild Eagle coaster was the new attraction being promoted at Dollywood in Pigeon Forge, Tennessee, in 2012.

A costumed character greets a guest during Kentucky Kingdom's first Halloween event, Hallowscream. At one time, Kentucky Kingdom was the closest major competitor to Cincinnati's Kings Island.

Riverside Amusement Park was a popular trolley park in Indianapolis. The park, home to the Thriller and Flash wooden roller coasters, closed in the early 1970s primarily due to issues with segregation.

The continued popularity of theme parks persuaded Taft Broadcasting to abandon a successful, old-style amusement park. Taft Broadcasting owned Coney Island on the banks of the Ohio River east of Cincinnati. Coney Island was firmly rooted in the Cincinnati community and drew patronage from surrounding states. The park offered a magnificent large pool, lake, and river amenities including a paddlewheel boat dock, and a beautiful grove of trees,

well-manicured grounds, and spectacular and well-maintained rides. From the outside, the park was everything a traditional park could be. However, numerous issues hindered the operation. Coney was landlocked, and frequent flooding discouraged future investment. The decision was made to close the park and to build a replacement in the suburbs. Kings Island opened in 1972 to rave reviews.

Walt Disney visited Riverside on his tour of parks around the country. Disney studied several parks to gain ideas for Disneyland. From Riverside, Disney liked the park's hub-and-spoke midway design. Instead of placing a carousel in the middle like Riverside, Disney placed a castle in the center of his park.

The Lake Como Railroad at Cincinnati, Ohio's Coney Island was a popular attraction. Elaborate scenes depicting early Native American and pioneer life could be found alongside the rails.

This promotional brochure for Cincinnati's Coney Island depicts the vibrancy and appeal of the traditional amusement park experience.

Built in 1926 by the Philadelphia Toboggan Company, the Grand Carousel is the oldest ride operating at Cincinnati, Ohio's Kings Island.

The Fun Parade at LeSourdsville Lake Amusement Park was a traditional funhouse. LeSourdsville was home to several funhouses and dark rides over the years, but fires ended this era of park history.

While most theme parks shunned their amusement park heritage, Kings Island embraced the best of what people loved about old, traditional parks. Theme parks typically shunned midway games of chance, but the general

public still loved to fork over money to be challenged by throwing a ball or shooting a basket. People loved the old rickety wooden coasters that were largely absent from competing theme parks. Taft Broadcasting persuaded master coaster designer John Allen from retirement to build the new Scooby Doo and Racer twin racing coasters. The Racer was the centerpiece of a Coney Island-themed area that paid homage to the vacated Coney Island. Coney Island closed after the 1971 season, and several rides were relocated to the new venue.

The new theme park industry saw themselves as a class above their smaller, blue-collar counterparts. But the old parks held tight to some degree of allure: Walt Disney is known to have visited many traditional parks when conjuring ideas for his mouse kingdom. Disney visited Cincinnati's Coney Island and was impressed by the park's cleanliness and general operations. He also visited Riverside Park in Indianapolis, adopting and modifying the park's unique hub-and-spoke midway layout. For the most part, parks had a central walkway with rides on either side of the midway. Riverside's circular walking footprint made sense to Disney, but instead of a carousel in the middle, Disney opted for a castle.

Cincinnati's Coney Island was a unique park that refused to die. After Kings Island opened, Coney Island remained in limited operation.

During the 2002 season, a carnival operator was hired to bring new rides to LeSourdsville Lake Amusement Park and perform maintenance on existing rides. Unfortunately, the relationship did not gel, and the park abruptly closed. This image was from across the lake was shot a few days before the park permanently closed.

FANTASY FARM MOTEL

Fantasy Farm was a small children's park located adjacent to and independent of LeSourdsville Lake Amusement Park in Middletown, Ohio. At the entrance to the park stood a motel, a forerunner to the modern amusement resorts of today.

The historic Sunlite Pool continued to provide relief from the sun, and eventually Zoom Flume waterslides were installed. The facility was renamed Old Coney and continued to provide the Cincinnati community with a gathering spot. As time progressed, additional attractions were added, including a separate admission film, *The Last Days of Coney Island*, shown on weekends in one of the old midway buildings, paddle boating on Lake Como, and picnic grounds capable of hosting large corporate events. A private vendor reintroduced steamboat rides down the Ohio River. The Moonlite Gardens ballroom began hosting elaborate events and local bands. The park went through ownership changes that brought a large outdoor performing arts center to the grounds, and eventually mechanical rides reappeared. Coney Island, the most famous of the park's previous names, was reinstated. The park was reborn and Coney Island forged on into the next century.

While Kings Island grew from the seeds of Coney Island planted a century earlier, other Cincinnati area parks would close within the shadows of the large theme park. LeSourdsville Lake Amusement Park, known as Americana in later years, was a popular traditional park on the outskirts of Middletown, Ohio. Although the park battled economics, including bankruptcy, ownership changes, and even a failed revival attempt, it could no longer compete with Kings Island and closed in 2002. Another Cincinnati park, Lunken Airport Playfield Kiddieland, closed in the early 1990s.

Meanwhile, Taft Broadcasting, riding the success of Kings Island, opened a sister theme park in Doswell, Virginia, named Kings Dominion (1974) and acquired Carowinds (1974), a park located directly over the North Carolina–South Carolina state line. The original Taft Broadcasting parks have gone through several owners, including the movie company Paramount, and the owners of Ohio's Cedar Point, Cedar Fair.

Above all else, the success of the Taft parks impacted the amusement industry in several ways. At Kings Island, people waited in line for hours to experience traditional wooden coaster thrills. Young kids waited in line to ride the Scooby Doo coaster, which indoctrinated future generations to the thrill of the midway's grand dame, the old wooden roller coaster. Traditional amusement park rides were present on the themed midways. After Kings Island's success, theme park operators became much more interested not only in their heritage, but in the old mechanical, traditional amusement park staples: Ferris wheels, carousels, scramblers, bumper cars, and the scream machines of the past. People still enjoyed these simple pleasures—pleasures that were no longer taboo.

The unique Sea Cycles attraction operated at the defunct LeSourdsville Lake Amusement Park near Middletown, Ohio. In order to survive difficult economic times, small parks were challenged to add creative new attractions on shoestring budgets.

LOST PARKS AND THOSE THAT REMAIN

THE ADVENT AND PROLIFERATION of theme parks made it difficult for small, often family-owned parks to compete. With high-profile theme parks and their multimillion-dollar attractions, traditional parks were forced to redefine and rediscover their strengths. With aging buildings and rides in need of repair, parks also were facing higher property valuations and corresponding taxes. Most urban parks became landlocked, and from the 1960s through the 1980s, many famous parks disappeared from the American landscapes. Chicago alone lost three parks during this time: Riverview (1967), Old Chicago (1980), and Fun Town (1982).

Chicago's Riverview Park was a great loss. The park was located in Chicago's North Center neighborhood and featured several coasters including the Bobs, Comet, Silver Flash, Fireball, and Jetstream. The park featured Aladdin's Castle funhouse, complete with intricate mazes, collapsing stairs, and a rotating wooden barrel. Another favorite was the Tunnel of Love dark boat ride, where young couples could steal a kiss. Riverview was the epitome of the classic American amusement park: seedy at times, yet alluring and adventurous. The demolition of the park resulted in 74 acres of prime real estate ready for development. Replacing the park was the Riverview Plaza shopping center, a commuter college, a police station, a manufacturing building, and Richard Clark Park.

Riverview is fondly remembered by native Chicagoans, many offering a special memory with mention of the park. Reminders of the park abound. At the corner of west Roscoe Street and Damen Avenue in Chicago, the Riverview Tavern houses memorabilia of the old park. The original Riverview carousel continues to spin at Six Flags over Georgia. Some park ride foundations are still visible to those who venture into the wooded part of the old Riverview property.

The most significant tribute to the park was the brainchild of Ralph Lopez, a former Riverview employee. In 1978, Lopez gathered fans of the old park for a meeting heavily emphasizing Riverview memories, and the result was the formation of the National Amusement Park Historical Association, which has

Opposite: Riverview was a staple for recreation in Chicagoland. This poster, advertising for concessionaires, proclaims that the park had no competition in the Chicago area, which was untrue. At one time, Chicago was home to several amusement parks.

The ticket booth from Youngstown, Ohio's Idora Park is seen in this museum display. Just like mementos from Savin Rock Amusement Park are found in the Savin Rock Museum, artifacts from parks are exhibited at museums across the country.

Funhouse favorite Laughing Sal, once a staple at amusement parks across the United States, has virtually disappeared. This Laughing Sal once greeted guests at Erieview Park in Ohio. She continues her life making special appearances at festivals in the area.

grown to include amusement park enthusiasts and parks from around the world. The Association's focus has expanded beyond the remembered gates of Riverview to include the celebration of American and international amusement park history. Through education and preservation efforts, the Association has acted to preserve myriad rides including the second Tilt-a-Whirl ever produced, the last remaining Teeter Dip ride, and one of America's last remaining Venetian Swings. The Association also acted to find a home for a 1936 Smith and Smith Chairplane ride and was instrumental in the recreation of the Zippin' Pippin wooden coaster, both of which are entertaining young and old alike at Bay Beach Amusement Park in Wisconsin. Members of the Association have donated thousands of dollars for preservation efforts across America. Founder Ralph Lopez said, "If we don't do something, nothing will be left. Amusement parks are the heart and soul of America."

While too many parks have been lost to detail, a few granddaddies deserve mention. Savin Rock, an amusement park in West Haven, Connecticut, located on the west side of New Haven Harbor, closed in 1967. This traditional park was a virtual goldmine for fans of classic dark rides and funhouses. Over the years, the park area was home to an original installation Old Mill (1900), a classic Pretzel (1920s), Bluebeard's Castle Funhouse (1922), a Mill Chutes (1925), Noah's Ark swinging boat (1925), Death Valley Funhouse (1937), Peter Franke's Fun House (1946), McDonald's Funhouse (1948), and an R. E. Chambers Laff in the Dark. Funhouses have virtually disappeared from the American midway due to safety and insurance concerns, while traditional dark rides are disappearing at a rapid pace. Memories of the park are preserved at the Savin Rock Museum.

Euclid Beach Park was located on the Lake Erie shoreline in Cleveland, Ohio's Collingwood neighborhood and closed in 1969. Of the seven wooden coasters that had operated at the park, the LaMarcus Thompson-built

Switchback Railway was the first and shortest lived. The park was home to the second Flying Turns ever built. The popular Beach Boys band wrote about the Flying Turns in their song "Amusement Parks USA." The park's Laughing Sal funhouse laughing lady still makes occasional appearances in the Cleveland area, and the park's Great American Racing Derby ride still operates at Sandusky's Cedar Point. The Euclid Beach Park entrance arch still stands and is under governmental protection. The Humphrey Company,

Remembering the Sights & Sounds of

EUCLID BEACH PARK

COMMEMORATIVE
PROGRAM AND MAP

SEPTEMBER 27, 2009

the 40th Anniversary of the Park Closing

Euclid Beach Park now is a nonprofit organization dedicated to the memory of Cleveland, Ohio's Euclid Beach Park. Even forty years after closing, memories of the park are celebrated by area residents. This event program with art by William Kless contains numerous pictures and a park map.

39

Amusement parks have been memorialized in popular music recordings. From "Amusement Parks USA" by the Beach Boys to 50 Cent's "Amusement Park," many beloved tunes have flourished on the radio. Pictured here is the cover to Freddy Cannon's "Palisades Park."

This is a birds-eye shot of New Jersey's famous, but defunct, Palisades Park. The large and popular salt-water pool can be seen in the upper left corner.

producers of popcorn-related gift items, also produces Euclid Beach Park-related nostalgic gifts.

Palisades Park was located in the New Jersey towns of Fort Lee and Cliffside Park. Palisades closed in 1971, ironically because it was too successful and could not provide adequate facilities on the available land. Parking and gridlock traffic were continual issues, and patrons were often denied entry to the park due to overcrowding. The park also came under attack for its policy of furthering racial discrimination. There were also questions regarding future ownership of the park due to the passing of owner Jack Rosenthal. His brother Irving was left to run the park, but he was in his seventies with no apparent heirs. Memories of Palisades Park

are kept alive by the Palisades Amusement Park Historical Society and Freddy Cannon's immortal song "Palisades Park."

Playland at the Beach, also known as Whitney's Playland, was located in San Francisco, California, along the Great Highway at Ocean Beach. Ceasing operations in 1972, Playland was home to coasters, dark attractions, and other mechanical staples. Aside from Santa Cruz Beach Boardwalk, all the major West Coast seaside parks have vanished. The land values for beachfront property caused the demise of most ocean parks. Playland Not-at-the-Beach preserves park memories as a nonprofit family entertainment center containing many park artifacts.

Far too many parks were lost during a span of three decades. But while each defunct park represents a tragic loss, several currently operating parks in the United States keep the spirit of the traditional midway alive.

Many traditional amusement parks watched as theme parks eroded and then seized the opportunity to learn from their bigger brothers and revitalize operations. While impossible to profile every American amusement area within the course of this narrative, there are several parks that deserve recognition.

The interior of Memphis, Tennessee's defunct Libertyland amusement park's 1999 promotional brochure displays a variety of attractions.

The New Tidal Wave Is Making A Splash!

Catch The TIDAL WAVE! Libertyland's newest action-packed thriller, The Tidal Wave, promises to be the biggest hit of the summer! It's the ride everyone is screaming for as it flips and turns you upside down over 20 feet above the ground. Our all day ride pass allows unlimited rides on great rides like the WipeOut, the Kamikaze, the Sea Dragon, the Zippin Pippin, the Double Water Slide, the Log Flume and many, many more!

GAMES GALORE! Libertyland's games area is a great place to let loose and feel like a winner! Our new water race game and our new Skatterballs game add prize-winning action to your family fun. The more you win, the bigger the prize. So enjoy rows of skeeball, lots of video games and much more — all waiting to challenge you!

REVOLUTION TURNS 20! The Revolution, Libertyland's double corkscrew loop steel coaster, has been one of Libertyland's most popular attractions since 1979!

LIVE SHOWS! Twist and turn and laugh yourself silly at Libertyland's all-new FREE stage shows! This season debuts "The Great American Duck Race" in Quack Theater with family-style excitement and audience participation as live ducks race for the finish line. Dancing in your seat is required as the cast of "Hit City '99" takes the stage at W. C. Handy Theater with a show featuring chart-topping pop hits. Another new-for-'99 show is "Neon Country" featuring foot-stompin' country hits from the rip-roaring opening number to the fabulous finale live from Liberty Theater!

FOOD TREATS! Libertyland's '99 season brings exciting new treats like frozen cotton candy, flavored pretzels, and a new taste sensation, Dutch Dough - a fried bakery treat smothered in chocolate pudding or your favorite fruit topping. You can also enjoy carnival food like Pronto Pups, funnel cakes, cotton candy, Coca-Cola, hamburgers, nachos, ice cream and more at food stands and restaurants throughout the Park.

THE TIDAL WAVE RIDE THE ULTIMATE WAVE NEW FOR '99!

SPECIAL EVENTS! Libertyland's 1999 season is packed with tons of exciting events like special guest appearances, prize giveaways and great money-saving offers all season long. Call us for a list of our special weekend events!

Libertyland
Mid-South Fairgrounds • Memphis, TN 38104
http://www.libertyland.com

In Sandusky, Ohio, the once grand Cedar Point, known as the Queen of American Watering Holes, was almost dead by the late 1950s. However, under new ownership, the park began adding new themed areas and attractions in line with the offerings of larger theme parks, and by the 1970s, the park had regained and surpassed former glories. Aside from the numerous additions, the park repositioned itself as a resort with the goal of keeping patrons beyond a one-day visit. The publically traded company that now owns Cedar Point

At Martin's Fantasy Island on Grand Island, New York, special badges are given to spectators of the gunfights staged in the western-themed section of the park.

This assortment of amusement park memorabilia captures memories from the past, reminders of parks that have survived, as well as those no longer with us.

has not only expanded the park, but has purchased additional properties, growing annual revenue in excess of $1 billion.

Several parks maintained a traditional park atmosphere, capitalizing upon America's passion for nostalgia, but borrowing operationally from the theme parks. These parks have learned to market history. Pennsylvania's Kennywood is an example of a trolley park that transitioned the traditional park atmosphere into an environment of professionally dressed employees, immaculately clean midways, elaborate floral arrangements, live shows, and themed rides. While remaining a traditional park, Kennywood has borrowed operational ideas from the theme park industry without forsaking its traditional park roots.

Like Kennywood, many traditional parks have recognized the numerous advantages of being a small, traditional amusement park in a theme park world. These smaller facilities promote their locations as being close to home, not requiring miles of driving just to pull into an overpriced parking lot. The comparable cost of spending a day at a traditional park is far less than going to a theme park with inflated gate prices and overpriced souvenirs

This centrifugal force ride was on a pier overlooking Lake Schafer at Indiana Beach Amusement Resort in Monticello, Indiana. Ride placement is always a challenge given that the park sits on less than 20 acres.

Tom Spackman designed Superstition Mountain as a dark ride, coaster-like coal mine simulating experience. The Indiana Beach ride was a unique hybrid that answered the competition. This image shows construction of the unique elevator lift for the revamped ride, dubbed the Lost Coaster of Superstition Mountain.

and food. Small parks also know their communities and can cater to the needs of the neighborhoods in which they are situated. For example, Kennywood offers educational programs to school children and hosts ethnic days, band competitions, and festivals. The park has added a Halloween event with haunted attractions and reopens for the Christmas holiday with a fantastic light display, special foods and souvenirs, festive entertainment, and a visit from Santa.

Another traditional park that has survived is Indiana Beach, located on Lake Shafer in Monticello, Indiana. Park founder Earl Spackman came to the newly created lake to build a vacation home for his family. The lake, although beautiful, did not have a proper shoreline; instead it was encased by steep banks and cliffs. Spackman heard that Lake Shafer would be lowered to provide adjacent Lake Freeman with an ample water supply, a development that prompted Spackman to work within the community to create a beach. Using primitive tools and shovels, hauling dirt by horse and wagon, a beach took shape, a bathhouse was built, and a small refreshment stand was constructed. In 1926, Spackman's Ideal Beach was open for business.

This classic Indiana Beach newspaper ad promoted various aspects of the resort. Mascot I. B. Crow, seen at the upper left, is known for proclaiming that "There is more than corn in Indiana."

Within a year, the park ordered and installed a pair of toboggan slides rising 30 feet into the sky. With no master plan but the desire to grow, Spackman began to add attractions on the small tract of land he owned. Noticing a busy ballroom across the lake, Spackman decided to build his own ballroom, a move that proved popular during the heyday of the big bands—so popular that the ballroom, still in use today, was expanded twice.

Growth remained stagnant during the years until Earl passed away, leaving the park in his son Tom's able hands. Tom added the first rides to the park including a Ferris wheel, carousel, and Roll-O-Plane. In 1950, Tom changed the name to Indiana Beach, and rapid expansion followed.

Indiana Beach has since grown to include six roller coasters, a funhouse and dark ride, boat excursions, numerous flat rides, a hotel, vacation cottages, and campgrounds, making the facilities a true resort destination. As the park grew despite limited expansion space, many rides were intertwined and a few attractions were built on small piers over Lake Shafer. There was simply not enough room to build a wooden roller coaster, the Hoosier Hurricane, so the park built its first major coaster on steel beams over the water and existing midway. "People come back because we don't change anything people like, yet we keeping adding stuff," said Tom Spackman, Sr. "People come here for a reason. They like what's here. So why would we need to change anything except to improve something or add a new ride?"

Similar to Indiana Beach, one of the best-loved traditional amusement parks in America is Knoebels Amusement Resort in Elysburg, Pennsylvania. Nestled along a stream in a thick grove of trees, Knoebels had humble beginnings as a lumber mill business with land well suited to farming and recreation.

The park began as a community gathering place. A cool stream running through the property allowed opportunities for swimming. Tally-hos and hayrides were frequently scheduled, and picnicking was allowed on the grounds. In 1926, a proper swimming pool was added along with the park's first ride, a steam-powered carousel. A restaurant and a few simple games also opened during the first season.

Since then, the park has experienced tremendous growth due to the hard work of the Knoebel family—and to the dedication of its patrons. Park enthusiasts constantly point to the park's bumper cars as being America's best. Unique to the park is an award-winning dark ride, the Haunted Mansion, opened in 1973. Another in-house project was the relocation of San Antonio's defunct Playland Park's Rocket wooden coaster in 1985; the coaster was aptly named the Phoenix. In 1998, Knoebels embarked on rebuilding a classic lost roller coaster ride, Mr. Twister, from the defunct Elitch Gardens. Based upon the original plans, the ride was

This view of Knoebels Amusement Resort shows the wooded grounds of the park. The Crystal Pool, Twister wooden coaster, and other rides are clearly visible.

Pennsylvania's Waldameer Park is home to two classic dark attractions, a rarity in today's amusement parks. Developed by creator Bill Tracey, the Pirate's Cove walkthrough attraction is one of two known in existence. This walkthrough has changed very little over the years.

designed and built by Knoebels staff and local tradesmen; Knoebels's newest coaster opened on July 24, 1999.

Knoebels takes great pride in rescuing rides from defunct parks. The Black Diamond, opened in 2012, is a dark ride coaster that was rescued from demolition from an amusement pier in New Jersey and is yet another example of Knoebels's commitment to preserving amusement park history.

Quassy Amusement Park opened in 1908 and remains one of only eleven operational trolley parks in America. The park is nestled on Lake Quassapaug's south shore in Middlebury, Connecticut. The inland park, originally known for clambakes and picnicking, added numerous attractions throughout the years. Keeping modern, yet embracing traditional park roots, the park added the Wooden Warrior roller coaster in 2011, solidifying the future of this 20-acre recreational area. The park plans to continue adding family attractions, supplementing mechanical rides with water activities.

Waldameer in Erie, Pennsylvania, started as Hoffman's grove picnic area. The Erie Electric Motor Company, the city's premiere trolley service provider, leased the grove and renamed the land Waldameer in 1896. A dance hall was constructed and a carousel was added, with more rides, including three coasters, none of which survived. The year 1922 saw the addition of the beloved Ravine Flyer wooden coaster, later removed due to a major tragedy, followed by an investment in an Old Mill boat ride. Continual additions were made over the decades, the most notable being the 1951 Comet junior wooden coaster and the 1970s Whacky Shack and Pirate's Cove attractions. An expanded water park, as well as the installation of the Ravine Flyer II wooden coaster in 2008, guarantees the park will be around for years.

On August 5, 1879, a small lakeside picnic grove blossomed at the end of Rochester, New York's steam railroad line. While a few modest rides were added to encourage train ridership, Seabreeze Amusement Park continued to grow with the arrival of carousel concessionaires from Philadelphia, the Long family. Building on the popularity of the park's new carousel, future years saw the construction of four roller coasters, a classic Virginia Reel trackless gravity ride, and the world's largest saltwater pool.

In the 1940s, George Long, a third-generation member of the Long family, bought Seabreeze and renamed the facility Dreamland. One of the unique attractions created by the family was the 1963 Bobsleds, a wood-structured, Olympic bobsled-themed coaster with a steel tubular track. This highly popular ride fueled the addition of several new rides and eventually the return of the Seabreeze name. Solidly into its second century of fun, Seabreeze Amusement Park is America's fourth oldest park. The facilities have expanded to include a modern waterpark while preserving the traditional amusement park atmosphere.

Camden Park in Huntington, West Virginia, is the only amusement park in West Virginia. This park has survived a century of changes. Owner J. P. Boylin transformed a carousel at the end of a trolley line into one of the finest remaining examples of a surviving trolley park in America. The park contains a classic dark ride and an old wooden roller coaster. Still owned by the Boylin family, Camden Park remains popular with locals.

The mighty Jack Rabbit wooden roller coaster shares the midway with an antique carousel at Rochester, New York's Seabreeze Amusement Park.

Near Portland, Oregon, Oaks Amusement is one of the oldest continuously operated amusement parks in America. Another trolley park, Oaks still maintains a skating rink and picnic area alongside twenty plus mechanical rides.

New York's Midway Park, now part of the New York state park system, opened as a trolley park in 1898. As a swimming beach and picnic area, the park really became popular with the addition of the now-defunct Jack Rabbit roller coaster. The park is notable because a complete Herschell Kiddieland package still operates at the park. The original trolley depot still stands and houses the park's arcade.

Established in 1907 at the end of the Camden, New Jersey, trolley line, Clementon Park had the area's first nickelodeon movie theater. The theater complemented a large dance casino and other adult amenities. Early rides included a steam-driven carousel, and the Jack Rabbit wooden coaster was built in 1919. Through several ownership changes, the park grew to include a small water park and massive wooden roller coaster to replace the aging Jack Rabbit. Although located in Camden, an area known for high crime, the park stands as a safe oasis against a background of urban decay.

The Hudson, Pelham & Salem Railways introduced Canobie Lake Park within two months of opening their new trolley line. Canobie began operations in Salem, New Hampshire, in 1902. The park resembled a botanical garden, and area residents rode the trolley to the park sporting their finest outfits. Early patrons enjoyed canoeing and outdoor sports, picnicking, a penny arcade, and the gentle Circle Swing. By the late 1920s,

Natural features of the land were often incorporated into park names. This classic gateway to Oak Park in Sacramento, California, harkens back to bygone years; early amusement parks took great pride in their landmark entry arches.

49

Clementon Amusement Park in New Jersey is a traditional amusement park that caters to the family market. The park was home to one of the oldest operating coasters in the United States, but the coaster was unable to meet modern standards and was replaced.

the last trolley rolled through Salem, and the park closed on March 17, 1929. A local entrepreneur made wealthy by an electric paving business purchased and reopened the park in 1932. From Lakeview Park in Waterbury, Connecticut, the Greyhound roller coaster was purchased and reconstructed in 1936 and renamed the Yankee Cannonball. Current ownership consists of three friends working with an active management team to ensure the park's continued longevity.

Just outside the city limits of Bowling Green, Kentucky, Beech Bend Park is an amusement complex featuring a campground, racetrack, and amusement park. The park dates back to the 1880s on land covered with beech trees adjacent to a swooping bend in the Barren River. Early attractions included a pony ride, skating rink, dance hall, swimming pool, and bowling alley. It was not until the 1940s that Beech Bend Park experienced rapid growth with the installation of numerous rides.

In the 1970s, due to increased competition from theme parks, including Tennessee's Opryland to the south, the park fell into disrepair. Owner Charles Garvin was not in great health, and in 1979 the decision was made

to close the park (the racetrack remained open, however). The park grounds were acquired by country music singer Ronnie Milsap and associates, but the ownership group failed with park operations and ownership was reinstated to Garvin's heirs.

Beech Bend Park experienced several announced but false comebacks, and in 1984 the racing facilities were purchased by capable owners Dallas and Alfreda Jones. The park began hosting national drag racing and hot rod events that became so successful the couple purchased the rest of the land. Within a few years, the husband and wife team began reclaiming the park from damage done over years of neglect. The owners reopened the campground and pool, later gradually adding rides as funds became available. Park management made a true commitment to the park when the Kentucky Rumbler wooden coaster opened in 2006 to rave reviews.

New Hampshire's Canobie Lake Park is home to the Yankee Cannonball wooden roller coaster. This is one of the first major coasters successfully relocated from a defunct park.

At Pennsylvania's Conneaut Lake resort area, an early attraction, the excursion boat *Pennsylvania* (left), pulls into docks at the Bessemer Railroad Passenger Boat Pier on the south shore. The *Outing* passenger boat, along with two ice houses, is seen near the docks.

Aside from an eclectic collection of rides, the property is home to a Chance Sea Dragon swinging boat ride that came from pop star Michael Jackson's Neverland Ranch. The park has also greatly expanded their water park and entertainment offerings.

Conneaut Lake Park in Conneaut, Pennsylvania, was originally known as Exposition Park when it opened in 1892. The park is intertwined with the town of Conneaut Lake and features a boardwalk, sandy beach, and grand hotel. Hotel Conneaut has been preserved and is an excellent example of lake resorts that at one time were scattered around America. The wrap-around hotel porch still sports rocking chairs. The rooms are not climate controlled, and most bathroom facilities are shared European-style. Board games are available in the lobby, but televisions and individual room phones are not offered amenities.

The park itself was always modest in offerings. Aside from Hotel Conneaut, the Dreamland Ballroom was the major draw in the early years. Although coasters were added in the past, the park completed construction on the Edward Vettel-designed Blue Streak in 1938, which became the park's signature attraction. Fairyland Forest opened in the 1960s, but was later closed to develop a camping area. The park has always maintained a mix of carnival midway rides, but rare rides on site include an old Tumble Bug, one of two operating in the United States, and a gravity-powered dark ride complete with an infamous wall of chewing gum.

The crowded midway at the Pike in Long Beach, California, was a popular place. Among the rides, a whip and a large slide were curious attractions during the time. Santa Cruz Beach Boardwalk is the last remaining seaside park on the West Coast.

Some of the Amusements on the Pike, Long Beach, Cal.

Bay Beach Amusement Park in Wisconsin rests at the mouth of the Fox River on the east bank of Green Bay. The park dates back to the 1890s and originally offered a swimming beach in the days before the bay waters became polluted. A grand pavilion was built and remains the oldest structure on the property. The park is family friendly with most rides costing a quarter. There is a small-scale passenger train, bumper cars, a Ferris wheel, a giant slide, and an assortment of carnival and children's rides, including the historic and restored Chairplane circular swing. The park relocated the Zippin' Pippin wooden coaster from Tennessee in 2011, resulting in a massive increase in attendance. Several additional acres of land west of the park were purchased in 2006 and planned for expansion. This scenic park remains a perennial favorite with locals. Bay Beach Amusement Park is unique in that it is owned and operated by the city of Green Bay.

Santa Cruz Beach Boardwalk is the last remaining major traditional amusement park on America's West Coast. Located alongside a mile of sandy beach, the Beach Boardwalk offers an unmatched collection of modern and classic rides rivaling the Playland at the Beach in San Francisco and the Pike in Long Beach, both long gone and redeveloped. The Boardwalk is family owned and operated and has been in operation since 1907, but the history of the Santa Cruz amusement area dates back to 1865.

While not a proper park, Belmont Park in Mission Beach, California, offers a handful of attractions. The Giant Dipper roller coaster is one of only two classic wooden coasters operating on the West Coast. Built in 1925, the coaster has been restored and continues to thrill riders.

Miracle Strip Park
in Panama City
Beach, Florida,
closed in 2004.
This successful
and much-loved
seaside park was
home to a large
wooden coaster
and themed rides.

John Leibrandt is credited with opening the first public changing rooms on the beach. With the success of Leibrandt's investment, other bathhouses were constructed and concessionaires began developing the area. Promoter Fred W. Swanton initiated plans for a boardwalk and casino, envisioning the beach at Santa Cruz as the Coney Island of the West. Swanton was successful at building a massive casino that opened in 1904; the original building was destroyed by fire, however, in 1906. Along with renowned architect William Weeks, plans were made to rebuild a casino, only this time the development would include a ballroom, a swimming pool, an entertainment pier, and a boardwalk.

Shortly after the new facilities were built, the Boardwalk's first thrill coaster was built in 1908, the L. A. Thompson Scenic Railway, a four-minute mile-long ride. The year 1911 saw the addition of a Charles I. D. Looff merry-go-round and an 1894 Ruth Und Sohn band organ, both of which are still operating; the brass ring machine also still operates. The Scenic Railway was replaced in 1924 by the Giant Dipper wooden coaster, still the visual centerpiece and most popular ride on the midway.

The park continued to add rides and attractions, but the pool closed in 1963, replaced with a miniature golf course. In 1967, the Sky Glider

1963 **MIRACLE STRIP PARK** **2004**

12000 Front Beach Road • Panama City Beach, FL 32407
(850) 234-5810 (850) 234-0368
Email mspswiinfo@aol.com
www.miraclestrippark.com / www.shipwreckisland.com
Starliner Roller Coaster

was installed, a scenic overhead ski lift ride that doubled as a people mover. The 1970s saw rapid expansion and new rides, but a truly successful business decision was made in the early 1980s when the Coconut Grove banquet and conference facilities opened. The conference center brought a stream of people to the boardwalk who might otherwise not visit.

While the park suffered damage as the result of the 1989 earthquake that shook the San Francisco area, repairs and upgrades were quickly made as the Boardwalk entered the next decade. The Hurricane coaster, the park's fifth, replaced a twenty-year-old Jet Star coaster in 1992. The park expanded with the acquisition of the Surf Bowl bowling center across the street. In 2000, the park returned the original but updated and expanded Cave Train dark ride to operation.

Santa Cruz Beach Boardwalk remains a popular tourist destination, as well as a lasting reminder of all that has been lost along America's West Coast. President of the Santa Cruz Seaside Company Charles Canfield has stated that the Boardwalk is successful because the owners take great effort to blend vintage with modern attractions. The family atmosphere keeps people coming through the gates in record numbers.

This early 1970s postcard features a Boardwalk image of Atlantic City, New Jersey. An extremely rare Turbo ride is seen towering above the elevated train; only twenty-three Turbo rides were ever made.

WHAT NEXT?

ALTHOUGH a great number of special parks have disappeared from the American landscape, the U.S. amusement industry remains robust. It is nevertheless disheartening to hear about a park closure, but the pace of loss has slowed tremendously. Visiting the remaining parks becomes a celebration of a simpler past.

While theme and traditional parks coexist with the American amusement park industry, few new parks are being built. It appears the theme park market has reached a saturation point, given that most major markets are within a few hours' drive of a theme or traditional amusement park. Still, a handful of successful parks were constructed in the late 1980s and beyond, including San Antonio's Sea World Texas (1988), Wild Adventures (1991) in Valdosta, Florida, and Legoland in California (1999) and Florida (2011). On the opposite end of the spectrum, Hard Rock Park was built in Myrtle Beach, South Carolina, and opened in 2008, closing shortly thereafter. While an attempt was made to reopen the park as Freestyle Music Park, those efforts were short-lived and the park stands vacant.

Located in Saco, Maine, Funtown Splashtown USA evolved from a roadside drive-in restaurant in 1959 to an early family entertainment center with a few rides and later a full-fledged traditional park. Depicted is the heavily themed entryway to the park's Excalibur wooden coaster.

Large American theme park operators have expanded their international offerings with new parks and partnerships, while existing parks continue to expand and upgrade facilities, hoping patrons will extend their visits and spend more money at their parks. This trend appears likely to continue.

Competition is not so much between theme and traditional amusement parks, but all entertainment options available within the marketplace. A day at the park is in competition with television, movies, video games, live music concerts, outdoor recreation, and other options that vie for our precious leisure time. Even with coupons and park promotions, a day at the park costs a pretty penny or two.

The economy also plays a factor in park success. If people are employed and earning a paycheck, they will eventually spend money on leisure activities. With rising gas prices, Americans are opting to travel less, exploring leisure options in their own communities. Family entertainment centers, which are small versions of amusement parks, exist in most communities. These centers may include arcades, climb areas, spray parks, miniature golf, bowling, go-carts, bumper boats or cars, and possibly a handful of mechanical rides or attractions.

Like family entertainment centers, water parks prosper in the wake of new economic realities. Water parks are facilities that contain a mix of pools, slides, and other water play elements. Orlando's Wet 'n' Wild was

The Pigeon Forge, Tennessee, Thunder Eagle wooden roller coaster is seen under construction. Shortly after opening, the coaster was closed and relocated to another park. Race World folded under fierce competition from the Dollywood theme park and other area attractions.

America's first water park, opened in 1977, and was the catalyst for additional free-standing water attractions. Geauga Lake in Aurora, Ohio, was the first amusement park that built a water park within the park to complement the dry ride offerings. Now most major theme parks, and many traditional parks, have water parks included as part of their gated offerings or a separate gated attraction. Large water parks continue to be built; however, local municipalities are investing in small aquatic centers that offer many of the same amenities without the large crowds and costly admissions of a destination water park.

Ride simulators from the 1980s were basically moving seats with wrap-around video images. The opening of *Star Wars* movie-based Star Tours at Disneyland took ride simulation to the next level. Industry experts touted the new technology and predicted that ride simulations would replace the real amusement ride experience. This supplanting of traditional amusement park rides by simulators has not occurred. People still like hopping on an old wooden coaster or taking a whirl in an antique auto. Still, ride simulations and virtual environments heighten sensory awareness and are becoming staples at theme parks around the world. The Harry Potter attraction at Islands of Adventure in Florida has taken the virtual experience to new heights. More virtual rides, or at least a blend of traditional and virtual methods, are in the planning stages.

The advent of the modern shopping center saw a handful of facilities expanding their entertainment offerings with the addition of amusement rides. Shoppers' World in Framingham, Massachusetts, was an early mall development constructed to include an amusement area.

Pennsylvania's Twin Grove Park was an amusement park that became a campground. Then, over the years, the campground began adding family attractions to the grounds to again include a small ride park. This simple twirling device only uses momentum generated by riders.

Pennsylvania's Idlewild began as a small, story-themed roadside attraction. The park has grown into a successful traditional/theme park hybrid. During the park's anniversary, banners claimed that "This much fun never gets old!"

Adventure parks offering rock climbing, ziplines, cliff diving, and other activities are being developed and are sure to be the next development craze. Mechanical rides are being installed in a variety of unlikely places including city parks and vacant lots, campgrounds, and shopping malls, the best example being the Mall of America in Minnesota. Fairs and carnivals also compete for America's limited leisure time and money.

Yet American amusement parks are as popular as ever, with many parks exceeding projected attendance. The coaster and thrill ride arms race to build the tallest, fastest, or most novel thrill machines is subsiding. Building new rides is costly, and with an aging population, more emphasis is being placed on creature comforts, entertainment, and retail. While grandma and grandpa may not want to ride the new coaster, they probably would enjoy a stroll down the midway, a nice dinner, and a show.

The hum of the neon lights still glow under a full moon. The coaster track is greased, and the carousel is spinning, the bass of the band organ thudding and the challenge of catching the brass ring just footsteps away. Young lovers float down the manmade river into the tunnel of love. Young children scream with delight as they make their way through the funhouse. Walking down the brightly colored midway, reality slips away, replaced by the magic of childhood, and fond memories are lived once more.

This map depicts the numerous attractions at the largest enclosed amusement park in America. Camp Snoopy was the centerpiece of Minnesota's Mall of America when the facility opened.

PLACES TO VISIT

Bay Beach Amusement Park, Green Bay, Wisconsin
    Website: www.ci.green-bay.wi.us/BayBeach
Camden Park, Huntington, West Virginia
    Website: www.camdenpark.com
Canobie Lake Park, Salem, New Hampshire
    Website: www.canobie.com
Coney Island, Brooklyn, New York
    Website: www.coneyislandfunguide.com
Idlewild Park, Ligonier, Pennsylvania
    Website: www.idlewild.com
Indiana Beach, Monticello, Indiana
    Website: www.indianabeach.com
Kennywood Park, West Mifflin, Pennsylvania
    Website: www.kennywood.com
Knoebels Amusement Resort, Elysburg, Pennsylvania
    Website: www.knoebels.com
Quassy Amusement Park, Middlebury, Connecticut
    Website: www.quassy.com
Sandy Lake Amusement Park, Carrollton, Texas
    Website: www.sandylake.com
Santa Cruz Beach Boardwalk, Santa Cruz, California
    Website: www.beachboardwalk.com
Stricker's Grove, Ross, Ohio
    Website: www.strickersgrove.com

ENTHUSIASTS' ORGANIZATIONS

American Coaster Enthusiasts (ACE)
    Website: www.aceonline.org
Dark Ride and Fun House Enthusiasts
    Website: www.dafe.org
Dark Ride and Fun House Historical Society
    Website: www.laffinthedark.com
National Amusement Park Historical Association
    Website: www.napha.org
National Carousel Association
    Website: www.nca-usa.org
A variety of regional clubs in the United States address specific target
audiences. These include Florida Coaster Club; Great Ohio Coaster Club;
Mid-Atlantic Coaster Club; Western New York Coaster Club; and a handful
of others. Most operating and many defunct parks have dedicated websites.

FURTHER READING

BOOKS

Adams, Judith A. *The American Amusement Park Industry: A History of Technology and Thrills*. Boston, Massachusetts: Twayne Publishers, 1991.

Cartmell, Robert. *The Incredible Scream Machine: A History of the Roller Coaster*. Fairview Park, Ohio: Amusement Park Books, 1987.

Cook, Richard, and Deborah Lange. *Glen Echo Park: A Story of Survival*. Bethesda, Maryland: Bethesda Communications Group, 2000.

Fried, Frederick. *A Pictorial History of the Carousel*. Vestel, New York: Vestal Press, 1964.

Futrell, Jim. *Amusement Parks of Virginia, Maryland, & Delaware*. Mechanicsburg, Pennsylvania: Stackpole Books, 2008.

Griffen, Al. *Step Right Up Folks*. Chicago: Henry Regnery Company, 1974.

Jacques, Charles J., Jr. *Kennywood ... Roller Coaster Capital of the World*. Vestal, New York: Vestal Press, 1985.

Kyriazi, Gary. *The Great American Amusement Parks*. Secaucus, New Jersey: Citadel Press, 1976.

Mangels, William F. *The Outdoor Amusement Industry*. New York, New York: Vantage Press, 1952.

McCullough, Edo. *Good Old Coney Island*. New York, New York: Charles Scribner's Sons, 1957.

O'Brien, Tim. *The Amusement Park Guide*. Old Saybrook, Connecticut: Globe Pequot Press, 2003.

PERIODICALS

ACE News. 1981 to present. American Coaster Enthusiasts, 1100-H Brandywine Boulevard, Zanesville, Ohio 43701-7303.

Amusement Park Journal. 1979 to 1987. Amusement Park Journal, P.O. Box 478, Jeffersonville, Ohio 44047-0478.

NAPHA News. 1978 to present. National Amusement Park Historical Association, P.O. Box 871, Lombard, Illinois 60148-0871.

INDEX

Page numbers in italics refer to illustrations